FRAGMENTS

7 Days of Fixing Fractured Faith

RAINAH DAVIS

DEVOTION II

Book Project Management by
Raindrop Creative, Inc. | StartWrite Publish Team

Editorial Team:
Gerald C. Simmons | Tiara Brown | Cherie Graham | Jennifer Eiland

Cover Art:
Raindrop Creative Design Team

978-1-970179-90-3 Paperback
978-1-970179-91-0 eBook

This book is a part of the *Activate Your Faith* Devotional Series.

Activate Your Faith:
The Art of Facing Fiery Trials

978-1-970179-77-4 Paperback
978-1-970179-04-0 eBook

The other two books in the series are:

Faith Foundation:
7 Days of Facing Fears and Overcoming Doubts

978-1-970179-90-3 Paperback
978-1-970179-91-0 eBook

Future Forward Faith:
7 Days to Believe Beyond Right Now for What's Next

978-1-970179-95-8 Paperback
978-1-970179-94-1 eBook

DEDICATION

To my husband – thank you for always having faith in me
and showing me that sometimes faith requires a fight.
To my parents – thank you for helping me find faith early
and praying for me unwaveringly until I believed for
myself.
To my children – may you find faith early, and never let it
go.
To my grandchildren – you are the manifestation of our
sincerest hopes and wildest dreams, don't drop the baton
of faith – pass to your children.

TABLE OF CONTENTS

PREFACE

Special note: If you have read the first devotional you can skip to the seven devotional days. This material is included for those new to the Activate Your Faith series.

This devotional has been rewritten three times. The version in your hands was the one God knew you would need at this time. The original chapters have been sliced and redistributed to teach you the art of facing every trial you face in the Activate Your Faith book series. The book is divided into three sections to clarify the different aspects of faith. Each week you will have a daily devotion that ties to a theme for that timeframe:

Week 1 – Section 1: Faith Foundation:
7 Days of Facing Fears and Eliminating Doubts

Week 2 – Section 2: Fragments of Faith:
7 Days of Fixing Fractured Faith

Week 3 – Section 3: Future Forward Faith:
7 Days to Believe Beyond Right Now for What's Next

The devotional in your possession are the first seven days of that 21-day devotional. I was compelled to make each section their own seven-day devotional, so you do not have to wait until the entire book is available.

Now, more than likely, you are grown. Therefore, I am not telling you what to do, and I would not dare try! I have five children over the age of 18, so I know grown people will do what they want (smile). However, I recommend you block off the next 21 days and go through the days in a quiet place. Also, I encourage you to do the activities at the end of each day.

I would love for you to do a personal mini-Bible study on the Biblical encounters and historical references that stand out to you. Studying the art of anything is to approach it from a multi-faceted level. Also, the art of facing trials with fiery faith sets you up strategically and psychologically to minimize damage and the wasting of resources. This knowledge is vital because before winning a battle, you must survive it first. Since in this life, we will face struggles, the idea is to meet each challenge in boldness and strength, relying on your faith in God. This book will serve as a powerful tool in your arsenal against the fiery trials attempting to quench your faith.

AUTHOR'S NOTE

A s I write the third intro to this book, I am in awe of the providence and timing of God. Six years ago this month, I was released from my job. As the days passed and months rolled in and out, it would be years before I understood why God would have allowed that event to occur.

Maybe you, like me, are staring at the face of a fiery trial in real-time. If so, then I have good news for you. There is an art to facing fiery trials. The way a pianist's fingers glide over the ivory keys or a relay runner completes a good baton handoff during track and field events is the same type of rhythm and execution needed to activate your faith.

I am in the midst of another transition as I pen these words to you. God has burdened me to complete this book in this specific season. Many of the personal stories you will read in this work are years old, but the principles I learned and will share with you are sound. It is an honor to join arm and arm with you through the fire. I assure you that the Lord is with us, and when we come out, there will not be a hint of smoke on us. I love you, and I am cheering for you. So, let's get started!

-     *Rainah*

INTRODUCTION

<u>Special note</u>: If you have read the first devotional book, *Faith Foundation*, you can skip to the seven devotional days. This material (the Introduction, Trial Types, and Overcoming Temptation sections are included for those new to the *Activate Your Faith* series.

I started this devotional series almost ten years ago and have added to it every few years. Still, unfortunately, other projects have taken priority over it. In November 2019, I was blessed to see Todd Galberth, my good friend, brother, and the author of the *Activate Your Faith* foreword, create a dynamic worship experience for his live recording. Listening to him share his powerful testimony and the faith that it took for him to produce this anointed and majestic experience inspired me to complete this unfinished work.

I had just released another *Activate* book designed to educate and empower individuals to develop the mindset necessary to start their businesses. During Todd's recording, I realized that no matter what industry a person is in, it takes faith to step out and do something extraordinary with passion and guts! I was in awe as I remembered God had allowed us to remain connected for almost a decade. I met Todd at World Overcomers Christian Church, where we both worked. He was one of the church's dynamic worship leaders. I vividly recall worshiping and crying out to God during his worship sets. In truth, his energetic, anointed, and intense praise and worship services helped me make it through one of the worst storms of my life. Therefore, it seemed fitting to have him be a part of this book. Shortly after, I started working on the book but was halted again by the COVID-19 pandemic that shut down the entire world.

And here we are again; in the fall of 2022, Todd released a single to the album I mentioned above called *He Won't Fail*. The song ministered to me profoundly, and again I was prompted to complete this book. A few days later, I told my business coach about the book, and she challenged me to finish it in seven days. So, let's get to it!

WHEN GOD SAYS NO

In 2010, I faced the most difficult trial of my life—the burial of a marriage that had figuratively died, decayed, and rotted many years earlier. I spent years praying, fasting, and begging God to revive and resurrect a relationship that was no longer beneficial for me. Thankfully, God denied my requests and pleas in an obvious and final way. Although devastated, I yielded to the undeniable "No" that I had heard from the Heavens and began to prepare myself and my daughters for a move that was unexpected for them and unknown to me.

In December 2010, I stepped out on faith and moved into a tiny house with my four daughters, ages fourteen to five. However, praise be unto God; at first, we survived, and then we thrived. Today at the time of this writing, not only am I remarried, but I am also the absolute happiest I have ever been. For years, I battled against the depression that convinced me I would lose my mind. Seriously, the enemy had me convinced that I would eventually end up having what my grandmother used to refer to as "a mental breakdown," which would leave me locked up in a padded cell and wearing a straitjacket for the rest of my life. However, as the hit gospel duo so eloquently put it: "But He didn't see fit to let none of these things be…You keep on, keeping on, keeping me…"

(Artist: Mary Mary/Song: "Thank You"/2002 Incredible Album). God kept me and brought me out stronger than ever.

Now I have a testimony! The same way God kept me, He can keep you, as the old saints would say, "He'll keep you when you can't keep yourself!" God is a "keeper," and I have experienced His "keeping power," which is so astounding that I want to help you experience it, too.

During the next 21 days, my goal is to help you face whatever trials you are experiencing with fearless faith and abundant joy. The Book of James admonishes us in James 1, verses 2-4: "2 My brethren, count it all joy when you fall into various trials, 3 knowing that the testing of your faith produces patience. 4 But let patience have its perfect work, that you may be perfect and complete, lacking nothing."

Then in 1 Peter 4, verses 12-13 we read: "12 Beloved, do not think it strange concerning the fiery trial which is to try you, as though some strange thing happened to you; 13 but rejoice to the extent that you partake of Christ's sufferings, that when His glory is revealed, you may also be glad with exceeding joy."

The passage in James reveals that "the trial" truly has a purpose and that if we yield to the purpose of "this trial," we actually gain "perfection and completion." In 1 Peter, we are instructed not to be caught off guard when trials approach us because our partaking in suffering, as our Savior did, will result in our having "exceeding joy" once His glory is revealed. Hence, the Bible is clear that we should embrace trials. We should face fiery trials, knowing there is a purpose at the end of the tribulation.

Yet unfortunately, this directive is much easier said than followed. So, over the next 21 days, I want to help you develop the skill set to face your trials with fearless faith, knowing that God will bring you out of every difficulty you face. There is an art to facing trials, specifically the fiery ones that we believe were sent to take us out!

Before I give you a formula for enduring the test, I must inform you that there are different kinds of trials. The Word admonishes us that in all our *getting*, we need to endeavor to get an *understanding*. Understanding is often the difference between being able to endure something or break under the weight of the pressure produced by it.

There are three basic kinds of trials that you will face during your Christian walk:

1. **TRIAL TYPE #1**—Discipline from the Lord, based on previous sin or natural consequences based on unwise decisions.

2. **TRIAL TYPE #2**—Persecution and suffering for living a Christian life.

3. **TRIAL TYPE #3**—Attacks and temptation from demonic forces sent to distract or destroy you.

TRIAL TYPE #1

The first trial type is the easiest for a mature believer to accept. Every mature saint can recount decisions that have landed them in a devastating situation. Mature people of God who face financial difficulty because of mismanagement of money conclude that "satan didn't steal their rent money." Mature believers can admit that they spent it on "miscellaneous" items, which are frivolous or unplanned expenses that can be hard to pinpoint at the end of the budget cycle. This type of trial is a direct result of the individual's behavior, and there are consequences as a result. For example:

If you don't pay your rent or mortgage = You will no longer have a place to stay.

If you cheat on your spouse repeatedly = You will eventually lose your spouse.

If you miss too many days from work = You will lose your job at some point.

If you get too many speeding tickets and don't drive at safe speeds = You could ultimately lose your license, car, or life.

There are also spiritual consequences for sin. The Word warns us that the wages of sin are death. We must be diligent in making better spiritual decisions, so we don't jeopardize our relationship with Christ.

Many believers repeatedly find themselves in a cycle of chastening from the Lord or reaping the consequences of destructive life "choices." It is vitally important that we master sin and make good decisions because this is the only type of trial that we have control over in our lives. The other two are based on

God's permission or permissive will. Trial type is reduced or even eliminated based upon your decisions. I encourage you to stop the cycle of consequences with which you find yourself by asking the Lord to help you with your decision-making process. We will talk about this matter in more detail throughout this book.

TRIAL TYPE #2

The second type of trial we face is inevitable. John 15:18-20 (NIV) reveals: "If the world hates you, keep in mind that it hated Me first. If you belonged to the world, it would love you as its own. As it is, you do not belong to the world, but I have chosen you out of the world. That is why the world hates you. Remember what I told you: 'A servant is not greater than his master.' If they persecuted Me, they will persecute you also…"

This Scripture informs us that every believer will suffer because of their faith. It isn't popular preaching; therefore, many speakers and ministers do not adequately remind us of this spiritual "fallout," but it is still the truth. A relationship with Christ doesn't give you a "trouble-free life" pass. In fact, the more havoc you wreck on the kingdom of satan you may find that the attacks against you often increase. When this counterattack occurs, you must get closer to the Lord and ensure that you don't allow the trial to push you further away. In truth, once you reach maturity and are unshakeable in your Christian walk, the enemy will often attack you or those closest to you. "The weakest links" in your life will take hits designed to impact or stop you. These types of attacks usually accompany the last kind of trial.

TRIAL TYPE #3

The third type of trial we face is the kind that makes us the most upset and is the most often assumed. When we first receive salvation, we believe that every challenge comes from our adversary, satan. However, as we mature in Christ, we learn that everything is not of the devil. Yet, because we know that even Jesus was tempted by satan, the enemy is coming for us. The Word defines satan's assignment quite specifically is to "kill, steal and destroy."

This assignment does not need any more defining and doesn't leave much to the imagination. The old saints taught us that the Bible says, "*When* your day of evil comes," and not "*If* your day of evil comes," because each of us has a day of evil that will surely come.

The Bible is also explicit on how to handle this type of trial. There are so many verses that minister to us on how to overcome temptation. We will explore some of them more in-depth throughout our 21-day journey together.

TWO KEYS TO OVERCOMING TEMPTATION

In the following Scriptures, there are some main points I want you to meditate upon:

1 Corinthians 10:13 (ESV) - "No temptation has overtaken you that is not common to man. God is faithful, and He will not let you be tempted beyond your ability, but with the temptation, He will also provide the way of escape, that you may be able to endure it."

James 4:7 (ESV) - "Submit yourselves, therefore, to God. Resist the devil, and he will flee from you."

A. God will provide a way of escape from the temptation you face. I am amazed at how often God sends ways of escape to us that we choose to ignore. I am also throwing myself under the bus. If we are honest, we have all fallen short of the glory on this one! When He sends the interruption (like a phone call or knock at the door) right before you are getting ready to give someone a "piece of your mind," you should let yourself be interrupted. Please don't ignore the call or the knocking: yield to it. Often, some of the worst experiences we have faced involve an instance where an interruption occurred when we were getting ready to fall into temptation. Still, we ignored the interference that was sent to save us. When we submit ourselves to God and resist temptation, that temptation has no choice but to flee from us.

Ephesians 6: 10-13 (ESV) - "Finally, be strong in the Lord and in the strength of His might. Put on the whole armor of God, that you may be able to stand against the schemes of the devil. For we do not wrestle against flesh and blood, but against the rulers, against the authorities, against the cosmic powers over this present darkness, against the spiritual forces of evil in the heavenly places. Therefore, take up the whole armor of God, that you may be able to withstand in the evil day, and having done all, to stand firm."

B. God has given us armor, so we should put it on! Decide to be strong in the Lord because you are fighting against the armies of hell. God has given us all access to armor we can put on to withstand enemy attacks. This armor helps to protect you so that you can stand firmly, fight bravely, and win against all evil forces.

Now that you have a basic description of the types of trials we face and what God expects of us as we meet them head-on. Let's learn how to face these trials with fearless faith and then use our knowledge to help others to do the same. We will do this by learning about the different types of faith that our Biblical ancestors applied to the challenges they faced. Every kind of faith provides the art form of facing and overcoming fiery trials.

DEVOTION II

FRAGMENTS

[OVERVIEW]

If you follow me on social media (@rainahmdavis) or are on the mailing list*, you will notice the title of this section's devotion was designed strategically to represent the communication law officials get from kidnappers or serial killers on crime shows.

Is anyone a Law & Order fan? What about CSI, NCIS, FBI, or any variations of those series? Well, if you have ever seen any of those shows or a movie with police in it, you have seen a letter with magazine letter cutouts that form words.

Those messages are typically created to cause terror to victims and frustration to law enforcement professionals. But do you know what all of those shows have in common? The enemy is typically always captured at the end. Often it takes a few episodes or an entire season to catch them.

Well, that is the case today. The enemy has messed up. He let you live long enough to get to *Fragments: 7 Days of Fixing Fractured Faith*. This section of *Activate Your Faith* is designed to rescue you from the enemy that attempts to frustrate you, mock you, stress you, and scare you half to death.

This week we serve notice on the enemy of our soul and our faith that he is caught! He is defeated, and he no longer has control. We are fixing our fractured faith and will be strengthened after these seven days. Right now, I am right there with you guys. I have been chasing the enemy for a while myself, and now that he is caught, we can all rest easier. Let's fix our fractured faith!

*Don't miss a thing!
Join the mailing list: http://rainahdavis.com

DAY ONE
Faulty Faith

faulty | ˈfôltē | *adjective*
Working poorly or unreliably because of imperfections; mistaken or misleading because of having flaws or displaying weaknesses.

Faulty Faith Scripture

Numbers 13:2-3, 17-20, 23-33, NIV

"**2** Send some men to explore the land of Canaan, which I am giving to the Israelites. From each ancestral tribe, send one of its leaders." **3** So at the Lord's command Moses sent them out from the Desert of Paran. All of them were leaders of the Israelites.

17 When Moses sent them to explore Canaan, he said, "Go up through the Negev and on into the hill country. **18** See what the land is like and whether the people who live there are strong or weak, few or many. **19** What kind of land do they live in? Is it good or bad? What kind of towns do they live in? Are they unwalled or fortified? **20** How is the soil? Is it fertile or poor? Are there trees in it or not? Do your best to bring back some of the fruit of the land." (It was the season for the first ripe grapes.) **23** When they reached the Valley of Eshkol,[a] they cut off a branch bearing a single cluster of grapes. Two of them carried it on a pole between them, along with some pomegranates and figs. **24** That place was called the Valley of Eshkol because of the cluster of grapes the Israelites cut off there. **25** At the end of forty days they returned from exploring the land. **26** They came back to Moses and Aaron and the whole Israelite community at Kadesh in the Desert of Paran. There they reported to them and to the whole assembly and showed them the fruit of the land. **27** They gave Moses this account: "We went *into the land to which you sent us, and it does flow with milk and honey! Here is its fruit. **28** But the people who live there are powerful, and the cities are fortified and very large. We even saw descendants of Anak there. **29** The Amalekites live in the Negev; the Hittites, Jebusites and Amorites live in the hill country; and the Canaanites live near the sea and along the Jordan." **30** Then Caleb silenced the people before Moses and said, "We should go up and take possession of the land, for we can certainly do it."* **31** *But the men who had gone up with him said, "We can't attack those people; they are stronger than we are." **32** And they spread among the Israelites a bad report about the land they had explored. They said, "The land we explored devours those living in it. All the people we saw there are of great size. **33** We saw the Nephilim there (the descendants of Anak come from the Nephilim). We seemed like grasshoppers in our own eyes, and we looked the same to them."*

When your faith is fractured, it creates fragments, and we want to get those fixed. Think about a physical fracture. If you or your child has ever had one, you know it causes a significant disruption in life. I have grandsons now, and one of them, Joey, fractured his arm when he was just four years old. That was new for me. My daughters were athletes, but it took a while before we dealt with any broken bones. *Boys, though*? They introduced me to fractures early!

When Joey fractured his arm, he had to wear a cast. He couldn't move it or get it wet! As you can imagine this is terrible set of restrictions for an active four-year-old boy. It was torture for us all. By definitions a fracture limits mobility slows you down and prevents you from doing what you typically do.

The same is true for your faith. A fractured faith keeps you from moving freely in what God has for you. That is why we are focusing on making your faith whole again this week! You can't afford to be stuck. It's **GO** season, and you need your faith to be strong and mobile!

Today, we are addressing faulty faith, a sign of those fractures. Like the definition mentioned earlier, faulty faith is:

- **Working poorly or unreliably because of imperfections**
- **Mistaken or misleading due to flaws**
- **Weak and lacking strength**

Now, let's get into the Word. Do your best with these Old Testament names, but when in doubt, mispronounce with confidence! Numbers 13:1-2, NIV reads, "The Lord said to Moses, 'Send some men to explore the land of Canaan, which I am giving

to the Israelites. From each ancestral tribe send one of its leaders.'"
So, Moses followed God's command and sent twelve leaders to
explore the land.

The twelve spies explored the land for forty days and returned
with a report. Then, we read that the majority gave Moses a
discouraging account. Despite the abundant blessings, most spies
focused on the obstacles. While Caleb spoke highly of the land, the
others responded with fear. Then, they spread doubt amongst the
community and gave a bad report (Numbers 13:31-33).

Let's pause *there*. Anytime you start telling people how
you think others see you, it's a sign that your faith is faulty. Not
everyone chosen will have the same level of faith as you. Just
because someone starts the journey with you doesn't mean they
will finish it with you. Notice that all twelve spies were leaders,
but not all leaders had the same vision, resilience, or faith.

Don't be surprised if people you thought would make it with
you disappear. Winning is a choice. It depends on your sight
and perseverance. Some people can't see beyond the obstacles.
Imagine seeing a land so abundant that it takes two men to carry a
single cluster of grapes! Yet, ten spies focused on the giants instead
of focusing on God's promise. How often does this happen in
life? God gives you a promise, tells you something is yours, and
instructs you to move forward, but fear creeps in when you see
the challenges.

You might think, "Someone else is already doing this," "I'm
not skilled enough." or "The market is too saturated." However,
your calling is unique. I wouldn't be doing these devotionals if I
let fear stop me. There are more skilled people, but God called me
to do this uniquely. The same is true for you. People are assigned
to you and your family, your community, and your ministry. If you

don't step into your calling, they won't receive what God intended for them **through you**.

If you see the obstacles wrong, you'll see yourself wrong. The Israelites saw themselves as grasshoppers, even though God called them to dominate. When you don't see yourself correctly, you:

- **Diminish God's power**
- **Shrink your own capacity**
- **Believe lies about your worth and ability**

God called you to soar like an eagle, not scurry like a grasshopper! Therefore, this week, we are breaking free from faulty faith. God has given you dominion. It doesn't matter who's already in the land–if God called you *to* it, He called you to rule *in* it.

For example, years ago, I watched Bishop Jakes preach a message. He said, "It's hard to be big when little's got you." Therefore, don't let little get *you*. You serve a big God, worthy of big praise, who has promised you a land flowing with milk and honey. Though there are giants in the land, fix your faith like Caleb and know that the promise is yours for the taking. God will withhold nothing good from those whose walk is blameless.

Today, we are coming to fix your fractured faith. Every fragment of your faith will be whole by the time this series ends: no more casts, canes, or crutches. Your fracture heals this week. Your faulty faith is fixed in Jesus' Name. AMEN.

We have almost completed day one. The cast around your fractured faith is coming off. By the seventh day, you will be whole, healed, and walking in what God intended! Continue reading the Faulty Faith Notes below for inspiration. I love you all. Have a fantastic day!

FAULTY FAITH NOTES

1. **Everyone chosen will not have the same level of faith**. You will be surprised at the number of people who start out with you compared to the number that make it to victory. Example: my junior high class versus our graduating class.

2. **Everyone's faith cannot see past the obstacles.** Do you know the opposition or the opportunity? Can you see past the pain to activate your purpose? Can you overcome the distractions to reach your destiny? If you struggle to answer yes to any of these questions, we must fix your faulty faith!

3. **You will see yourself wrong when you don't see the obstacles right.** You will diminish God's ability and your capacity. You will see yourself as a grasshopper when He created you to be an eagle that soars.

FAULTY FAITH PRAYER:

Lord, please restore our faith. Give us Your vision. Help us take dominion over every area You have called us to. We declare that we will see the goodness of the Lord in the land of the living. We receive Your promises and will no longer let obstacles stop us. In Jesus' name, Amen!

DAY TWO
Fair-Weather Faith

fair-weather | fer ˈweT͟Hər | *adjective*
Only able to function in favorable conditions.

Fair-Weather Faith
Scripture Lesson

Mark 4:35-40, NIV

"35 That day when evening came, He said to His disciples, "Let us go over to the other side." 36 Leaving the crowd behind, they took Him along, just as He was, in the boat. There were also other boats with Him. 37 A furious squall came up, and the waves broke over the boat, so that it was nearly swamped. 38 Jesus was in the stern, sleeping on a cushion. The disciples woke Him and said to Him, "Teacher, don't you care if we drown?" 39 He got up, rebuked the wind and said to the waves, "Quiet! Be still!" Then the wind died down and it was completely calm. 40 He said to His disciples, "Why are you so afraid? Do you still have no faith?"

Fair-weather faith is a call to examine the foundations of our belief. Genuine faith is tested and proven in the storms of life, holding firm to God's promises even when circumstances are unfavorable.

The need to fix our fractured faith is crucial. Day two shows us that fair-weather faith only functions under favorable conditions. Think about fair-weather friends–they're only around when everything is going well. Similarly, fair-weather faith only works when the circumstances are perfect. Still, we can't operate like that in the body of Christ.

Now that we have clarified fair-weather faith let's examine the passage above. What stands out is that the disciples had been with Jesus all day, watching Him preach and teach a vast crowd. Yet, when the storm came, they panicked, much like the song by New Edition that sings, "*Sunny days, everybody loves them. Tell me, baby, can you stand the rain?*"

The disciples were in a relationship with Jesus. Still, when the storm hit, they frantically woke Him up, asking, "Do you care if we die?" Of course, Jesus cared about them. However, the very real winds that beat upon them caused fear to take over. They were in a rush to feel safe again.

No one enjoys the uncertainty of a storm. Storms are loud and violent, and thunder and lightning are scary. Boats capsize in storms, and people can be tossed aboard and drowned. The disciples forgot one crucial thing: the Son of God was on the vessel! They had witnessed Jesus perform numerous miracles before this moment (but isn't that just like us)!?

How many times does God come through in various ways in our lives? Yet, time after time, we need to be reminded. Fair-weather faith is a belief system that only works when we get what we want. It is a clear sign that our faith has not matured to the point that, come hell or high water, we will not stop believing that the Master of the Sea can calm the waters and silence the breakers again!

The question for us is: can your faith withstand the storm? Does your faith only work when conditions are favorable? If this message doesn't apply to you, store these words for later or share them with someone who may need to hear them. Even if your faith feels strong today, storms will come. We must be aware of the seasonal storms affecting us and begin to prepare accordingly.

For example, I used to work with a woman who wouldn't drive in the rain. My mother and mother-in-law don't like driving in the rain either–but they did it when they needed to, especially when they were younger. I can only think of the opportunities and special occasions they may have missed due to the fear of driving in those conditions. However, this woman had a system worked out and didn't have to drive in the rain. As a single mom of four, though, I couldn't relate. I didn't have the option not to drive in the rain. If it rained and my kids had to go to school or I had to go to work, I got in the car and drove. I couldn't let external conditions control what I had to do.

In the same way, we can't allow the storms of life to control how we respond. Just as I had to keep moving despite the rain, the disciples had to continue trusting in Jesus, even when the storm raged around them. Yet, amid the storm, they panicked and were afraid because Jesus was asleep. This story is a powerful illustration of what happens when we allow fear to dictate our actions, rather than trusting in the presence of Jesus. Likewise, you have too much to accomplish only to activate your faith when the sun is shining with no clouds in the sky!

Think about fair-weather faith another way. Why were the disciples afraid that Jesus was asleep? Do you remember the WWJD (What Would Jesus Do) movement? If Jesus was sleeping, we should've just done what He was doing: resting. The disciples had been with Jesus all day, yet they still didn't trust Him. Even though they'd witnessed His power firsthand, they let the storm shake their faith. Maybe you can relate. You may be experiencing a storm with water in your boat right now. Yet, you must understand that the Master is right there. You are not alone. What you need to do is what Jesus did: rest in Him. Jesus didn't give half-hearted rest; He was on a pillow, entirely comfortable.

The amount of time Jesus spent in prayer gave Him confidence because He was fully God yet fully man. He knew that the elements had to obey Him. It was a teachable moment designed not to scare the disciples but to show them they had nothing to worry about with Him on the boat. This Biblical example is a reminder for all of us–Jesus gets no glory if we die in the storm. He wants us to trust Him, rest in Him, and know He is in control. Let's follow His example and rest, no matter how rough the storm may seem.

When we lack confidence, it's usually due to not practicing and spending adequate time in our Word and prayer. Both action items worked for the Messiah and will work for us, too! He left a template that shows us how to have unshakable faith that withstands the inevitable tests and storms in our lives. So, ask yourself what is competing for your time and what adjustments are needed to spend more time building up your faith reserves.

Getting into God's presence isn't a rushed experience. It is where we connect daily, intentionally, and consistently. It will ease the burdens as we turn them over time and time again. You will gradually feel the atmosphere begin to shift. Shifting can happen in one day, in a moment that you are aware of, or it can just lift off of you as you realize that practicing His presence broke the heaviness.

Being still requires knowing who is in control. If we are in control, then we should be in a frenzy because our understanding is limited. However, if we surrender control to the One who is all-knowing, we rest in the reality that God will lead us and guide us to safety. The problem is that we want the outcome to be comfortable. Unfortunately, that is a condition of fair-weather faith.

When we allow the difficulty, we face to consume us, it indicates that we have failed to trust Jesus who is right there with us. The fact remains that He is not panicking about our situation. Take a deep breath, get in the presence of God, and rest knowing that all He needs to do is speak a Word, and the storm must obey! Peace–be still!

FAIR-WEATHER FAITH NOTES

1. **Fair-weather faith cannot withstand life's storms; it only functions under favorable conditions; it is fragile and unreliable.** As described in James 1:2-4, true faith is tested and strengthened through trials. Just as fair-weather friends only stick around during good times, fair-weather faith crumbles when adversity strikes. Genuine faith is resilient, built on trust in God, and can endure sunny days and storms.

2. **Rest in Jesus during the storm: the disciples panicked when the storm hit, even though Jesus was asleep in the boat with them.** Their fear showed a lack of trust in Him despite His presence. It illustrates the importance of resting in Jesus, even when external circumstances seem overwhelming. Instead of responding with fear and panic, believers should follow Jesus' example and trust that God is in control, just as He calmed the storm.

3. **Trials refine and strengthen our faith.** 1 Peter 4:12-13 and the story in Mark 4:35-40 highlight how challenges refine our faith. The trials believers face are opportunities to deepen their trust in God, share Christ's sufferings, and prepare them for greater joy when His glory is revealed. This enduring faith holds fast to God's promises, knowing He works all things for their good, even amid life's fiercest storms.

FAIR-WEATHER FAITH PRAYER

Lord, thank you for reminding us that you are a safe haven during our storms. May we release our fair-weather faith and embrace unshakeable, unmovable belief in You and Your abilities. Amen.

DAY *THREE*
Faltering Faith

Faltering |fält(ə)riNG | *adjective*
To waver, hesitate in purpose or action, become unstable, lose strength or momentum.

Faltering Faith
Scripture Lesson

2 Kings 5:1-15, NIV

*"**1** Now Naaman was commander of the army of the king of Aram. He was a great man in the sight of his master and highly regarded, because through him the Lord had given victory to Aram. He was a valiant soldier, but he had leprosy.**2** Now bands of raiders from Aram had gone out and had taken captive a young girl from Israel, and she served Naaman's wife. **3** She said to her mistress, "If only my master would see the prophet who is in Samaria! He would cure him of his leprosy."**4** Naaman went to his master and told him what the girl from Israel had said. **5** "By all means, go," the king of Aram replied. "I will send a letter to the king of Israel." So Naaman left, taking with him ten talents of silver, six thousand shekels of gold and ten sets of clothing. **6** The letter that he took to the king of Israel read: "With this letter I am sending my servant Naaman to you so that you may cure him of his leprosy."*

*ced of his leprosy? See how he is trying to pick a quarrel with me!"**8** When Elisha the man of God heard that the king of Israel had torn his robes, he sent him this message: "Why have you torn your robes? Have the man come to me and he will know that there is a prophet in Israel." **9** So*

*Naaman went with his horses and chariots and stopped at the door of Elisha's house. **10** Elisha sent a messenger to say to him, "Go, wash yourself seven times in the Jordan, and your flesh will be restored, and you will be cleansed."*

***11** But Naaman went away angry and said, "I thought that he would surely come out to me and stand and call on the name of the Lord his God, wave his hand over the spot and cure me of my leprosy. **12** Are not Abana and Pharpar, the rivers of Damascus, better than all the waters of Israel? Couldn't I wash in them and be cleansed?" So he turned and went off in a rage.*

***13** Naaman's servants went to him and said, "My father if the prophet had told you to do some great thing, would you not have done it? How much more, then, when he tells you, 'Wash and be cleansed'!" **14** So he went down and dipped himself in the Jordan seven times, as the man of God had told him, and his flesh was restored and became clean like that of a young boy. **15** Then Naaman and all his attendants returned to the man of God. He stood before him and said, "Now I know that there is no God in all the world except in Israel. So please accept a gift from your servant."*

W hat happens when your faith falters? When faith wavers, it hesitates in purpose or action and becomes unstable when it falters. It loses strength and momentum–and none of those things are good! You might wonder how this plays out in real life, so let me help you make the connection.

Picture this: a cargo ship or sea-faring vessel carries shipping containers filled with goods from merchants far and wide. Most are engineered to last upwards of twenty-five to thirty years or more if properly maintained. On March 26, 2024, a cargo ship named "Dali" headed to Colombo, Sri Lanka, carrying 1.5 million gallons of fuel and oil lubricant (approximately half its 95-ton capacity). Yet, it lost control due to a mechanical failure.

The ship crashed into the forty-seven-year-old Frances Scott Key bridge in Baltimore, Maryland. In the early morning hours, six people were killed, the port of Baltimore was disabled, and a dozen other vessels were trapped. The crash caused significant delays and congestion for six different ports on the East Coast and affected almost 8,000 jobs.

In addition, state officials estimated that the damages would likely exceed 1.7 billion dollars. The Army Corps of Engineers was perceived to take four years to repair and rebuild the bridge and surrounding infrastructure. Additionally, a National Transportation Safety report states that there were at least two complete blackouts the day before the vessel left the port. The third blackout would have proven fatal!

Similarly, faltering faith is a critical point in a believer's life that can lead to a similar collision and collapse. However, there are warning signs that you should take notice of. In the case of the ship losing power, the facts are that it was reported to have had shoddy repairs over time, which ultimately rendered the propeller, rudder, and bow thruster unable to engage appropriately in an emergency.

The propeller generates forward thrusts, the rudder controls the direction of the water flow, and the rudder allows for sideway movement. These components affect the propulsion, steering, and fine-tuning of the ship's movement, particularly in tight spaces (Taylor, C.,2024). None of these components would be present without a functional electrical system, and they would not help in a crisis!

In the same way, the foundation of our faith is in the disciplined daily reading of the Word of God and the exercise of its application. It seems like you've heard it all before until you are faced with circumstances that require fortitude and proper navigation in tight spaces. Ultimately, you must learn to move through life's expected and unexpected happenings. Please don't underestimate the power of faith; it can move mountains, including your situation!

Imagine with me if the Dali ship had followed the well-documented procedures, including performing routine maintenance and repairs. It would have saved six lives, more than a billion dollars, and four years of labor, to say the least! Remember that such vessels can operate for twenty-five to thirty years or more. The Dali was built and ready to sail in 2015; the ship was only nine years old! It hadn't reached its length of days yet. In a relatively short period, it suffered a catastrophic failure.

There are many reasons to review the areas in our lives where our faith has the warning signs that could, if left in a shoddy condition, lead to an outcome we don't want to see. But what causes faith to falter? What situations impact our faith in this way?

This chapter will look at God's Word for Biblical examples of the faith needed when life gets tough.

For instance, let's examine 2 Kings 5 above. These verses clearly show faltering faith versus complete faith in God's healing ability. In this account, we're introduced to Naaman, a high-ranking military officer–likely the equivalent of a colonel or lieutenant. Naaman was a man of great honor and favor before the Most High God of Israel. He was a capable and respected leader, but he suffered from leprosy. The other key figures in this story are:

- The *servant girl*, a maid in Naaman's household, boldly spoke his possible healing
- *Naaman's wife*
- *The King of Syria*
- *The King of Israel*
- *The Prophet Elisha*, a renowned servant of God and a protégé of Elijah, the tremendous miracle-working prophet
- *Naaman's servants*, who later played a critical role in his obedience to Elisha's instructions

The way this story unfolds teaches us a lot about faith. First, notice how the servant girl expressed confidence to Naaman's wife, saying that the prophet in Israel could heal him. Her faith and boldness set Naaman's healing into motion. Her simple statement caused others to act, eventually leading to the King of Syria sending a request to the King of Israel on Naaman's behalf.

Now, here's where things take a turn. The King of Syria sent the request to the King of Israel, but the King of Israel misunderstood it entirely. Instead of recognizing that God's power, not his own, would bring healing, he mourned unnecessarily, thinking he was being asked to perform a miracle himself. He failed to understand that the power belonged to God all along.

How often do we do this? Like the King of Israel, we panic or despair, believing the responsibility rests on us when, in reality, it is God who has the power to work in our situation. We mourn needlessly instead of trusting in His ability, which brings instability in our faith and ultimately causes it to falter, like the science project.

This misunderstanding impacted Naaman as well. Although he was a believer, his faith hesitated when Elisha gave instructions that didn't make sense to his natural mind. Instead of immediately obeying, he became angry and questioned the wisdom of the prophet's directions. He almost missed his blessing because of his arrogance and pride.

In contrast, we can learn from Naaman's servants. When Naaman resisted Elisha's instructions, his servants spoke up, encouraging him to obey–no matter how simple or insignificant the instructions seemed. Their faith-filled reminder led to Naaman's obedience, resulting in his healing.

This story offers us a profound lesson: faith is not about understanding everything perfectly or having all the answers. It's about trusting God enough to obey, even when the path doesn't make sense. When your faith falters, take a step back, reflect, and remember that the power to overcome isn't yours–it's God's. Stay anchored in His wisdom, trust His instructions, and allow Him to work miracles in your life.

The story of Naaman is one of my favorites, and as you can tell, I love the Old Testament. A couple of things about this story stand out to me. The first point is this: **you can be significant and**

still have a problem. This is especially important to remember as we navigate today's society and culture. There's this belief that if we land the right job, achieve a particular position, get married, buy a car, or reach a specific level of success, then we've "arrived." It's as if we expect that all struggles, challenges, and traumas will magically disappear once we reach these milestones. But that's not true.

If you live long enough, you'll realize you can be significant and still have problems. In this story, Naaman is a commander, a mighty soldier, and a noble leader who has won a substantial war for his country. By all accounts, he was a man of outstanding accomplishments. But even with all his greatness, **he had a problem: leprosy**.

The truth of life is this: you can be winning in one area and struggling in another. If we're honest, life often combines triumphs and trials. For example:

- You might have a great marriage AND a child who challenges you at every turn.
- You might have a fantastic child AND feel like dropping your spouse off a bridge (some days).
- You could be working at the best job you've ever had AND dealing with coworkers you can't stand.

The reality is this: **you will often win and face challenges simultaneously.**

The second point is equally profound: **your life may be disrupted on behalf of helping someone else**. In this story, Naaman's wife had a servant who was pivotal in his healing. This servant (despite technically being an enslaved person) was the one who spoke up and provided the instructions that ultimately led Naaman to his miracle. She was used as a vessel to bring him to healing (Ephesians 6:5-8).

However, let's consider the alternative. The servant could have reserved this vital information. She could have had an attitude and been bitter about her circumstances. She was, after all, taken from her homeland, and forced to serve in someone else's house. But instead, she stepped up. She said, "I know the man who can heal you. I know the one with the master plan." This example shows us that sometimes, even when life feels disrupted in a less-than-ideal season, **we can still be a blessing to help someone else.** That's the beauty of this story—God's plan often works through our triumphs and trials. Amen!

The third lesson we've learned today is this: **your faith can falter because of a particular delivery method or lack of preparation**. Are you upset or frustrated because your miracle hasn't come as expected? Are you clinging to the idea of "having it your way," like the old Burger King slogan? Sometimes, our faith falters because the outcome doesn't look like what we envisioned, or the blessing doesn't arrive as we thought it would. Or maybe the preparation needs an adjustment to avoid imminent destruction.

Whatever the case, don't be that person. Don't let your frustration with the delivery method cause you to miss your blessing. Obedience is the key to reaching the other side of your miracle, and it may require trusting a process that looks entirely different from what you imagined. Understand that what seems redundant and unnecessary could be precisely what is needed when your faith is tested.

We've all seen this happen—people get so stuck in their expectations that they overlook the blessing when it comes in an unexpected form. It's like the lesson from the book *Who Moved*

My Cheese? Change is inevitable and resisting it can hold us back. One of my children, for example, struggled deeply with change. She hated it, couldn't deal with it, and had to learn to adapt over time. I don't know where she'd be today if she hadn't.

In the same way, we have to let go of rigid expectations and learn to trust God, even when things don't happen as we thought they would. Sometimes, God intentionally switches things up to demonstrate His power and sovereignty. Look at Naaman's story– his condition became the very thing that led him to God.

Sometimes, the affliction we face is the pathway to a deeper relationship with Jesus. Often, it's through pain and perseverance that we come to know God on a whole new level. Growth doesn't always happen in sunshine and rainbows; it occurs in the valleys; on the other side of the trials, we endure. Following God's instructions positions us for deliverance even during pain.

So, I encourage you today: **don't let your faith falter this season. Your life and those around you could be permanently impacted**. Today, I pray for your healing, strengthened mind, and unwavering faith. I'm praying that you'll see beyond the method of delivery, beyond the circumstances, and that you will begin to trust God fully. He will bring you through; on the other side, you'll know Him in a way you've never known Him. **God will get the glory.** Amen!

FALTERING FAITH NOTES

1. **You can be significant and still have a problem.** Naaman was a commander and valiant soldier, but he had leprosy. You can win in one area of life and lose in the other. In every season, God is in control and will help you reach your blessing.

2. **Sometimes, your life will get disrupted to help someone else.** Naaman's wife had a servant captive from another place, but she was the vehicle God used to get him to his healing.

3. **Don't miss your miracle because you don't want to follow instructions.** Is your faith faltering or unsteady because of the method of delivery? Can you only accept the blessing the way you want it? Are you trying to treat the Kingdom of God like Burger King and *have it your way*? If so, you will fail every time. God is not a short-order cook. You have to obey His instructions, even when it is not what you want to hear or do. Don't make the mistake of missing your blessing because it is not in the package that you were expecting. Don't allow your faith to falter. You are too close to your miracle.

4. **Avoid a catastrophe**–there are no shortcuts in the Kingdom! Lessons can be learned from one of the worst ship crashes in ten years or so, as we discussed earlier. You will better navigate various situations and avoid many destructive outcomes through routine reading, studying, and applying the Word of God to your life. Notwithstanding, your faith will increase as you see the timeless truth of how to trust God, who has been faithful to perform His Word throughout history. Not on our timing, but in God's timing, His will be accomplished. Submitting to God takes patience, and, at times, long-suffering to see these results revealed.

5. **Faltering faith has warning signs**. It could appear that the Dali lost complete power with two subsequent blackouts the day before the crash and the warning sign that the vessel was unsafe to continue its journey. However, the report that uncovered many patchwork repairs was blamed for the ultimate "faltering" equipment mishap. We cannot skip around confronting this on our faith journey. We cannot be so busy that we fail to spend time with God and expect to endure navigating the waters of our lives. To make it safely to our destination, we must be intentional!

FALTERING FAITH PRAYER:

Lord, please reveal the areas in my life where my faith has faltered. I want to submit to your will and trust your plan for my life. May I never forget all the goodness You've shown me, and may I testify Your goodness wherever I go. Amen.

DAY *FOUR*
Fatigued Faith

Fatigued | fə-ˈtēgd | | *adjective*
Weaken by repeated variations of stress, extreme tiredness resulting from mental or physical exertion or illness, or a lessening in one's response to or enthusiasm for something; fatigue describes a physical, psychological, or social impairment that includes tiredness, sleepiness, reduced energy, and increased effort needed to perform tasks at a desired level.

Fatigued Faith
Scripture Lesson

1 Kings 19:1-18, NIV

"1 Now Ahab told Jezebel everything Elijah had done and how he had killed all the prophets with the sword. 2 So Jezebel sent a messenger to Elijah to say, "May the gods deal with me, be it ever so severely, if by this time tomorrow I do not make your life like that of one of them."

3 Elijah was afraid and ran for his life. When he came to Beersheba in Judah, he left his servant there, 4 while he himself went a day's journey into the wilderness. He came to a broom bush, sat down under it and prayed that he might die. "I have had enough, Lord," he said. "Take my life; I am no better than my ancestors." 5 Then he lay down under the bush and fell asleep.

All at once an angel touched him and said, "Get up and eat." 6 He looked around, and there by his head was some bread baked over hot coals, and a jar of water. He ate and drank and then lay down again. 7 The angel of the Lord came back a second time and touched him and said, "Get up and eat, for the journey is too much for you." 8 So he got up and ate and drank. Strengthened by that food, he traveled forty days and forty nights until he reached Horeb, the mountain of God. 9 There he went into a cave and spent the night. And the word of the Lord came to him: "What are you doing here, Elijah?" 10 He replied, "I have been very zealous for the Lord God Almighty. The

Israelites have rejected your covenant, torn down your altars, and put your prophets to death with the sword. I am the only one left, and now they are trying to kill me too."

11 The Lord said, "Go out and stand on the mountain in the presence of the Lord, for the Lord is about to pass by." Then a great and powerful wind tore the mountains apart and shattered the rocks before the Lord, but the Lord was not in the wind. After the wind there was an earthquake, but the Lord was not in the earthquake. **12** After the earthquake came a fire, but the Lord was not in the fire. And after the fire came a gentle whisper. **13** When Elijah heard it, he pulled his cloak over his face and went out and stood at the mouth of the cave. Then a voice said to him, "What are you doing here, Elijah?" **14** He replied, "I have been very zealous for the Lord God Almighty. The Israelites have rejected your covenant, torn down your altars, and put your prophets to death with the sword. I am the only one left, and now they are trying to kill me too."

15 The Lord said to him, "Go back the way you came, and go to the Desert of Damascus. When you get there, anoint Hazael king over Aram. **16** Also, anoint Jehu son of Nimshi king over Israel, and anoint Elisha son of Shaphat from Abel Meholah to succeed you as prophet. **17** Jehu will put to death any who escape the sword of Hazael, and Elisha will put to death any who escape the sword of Jehu. **18** Yet I reserve seven thousand in Israel—all whose knees have not bowed down to Baal and whose mouths have not kissed him."

It's already day four, and you're still rocking with me; *this is exciting*! I have much to share with you today, so grab a seat and get comfortable. Today, we are going to discuss fatigue and its common symptoms.

Fatigue is a state of being weakened by repeated stress, extreme tiredness from mental or physical exertion, or even illness. It is also described as a decreased enthusiasm or response to something over time. Fatigue impacts us physically, mentally, and even socially, leading to tiredness, sleepiness, reduced energy, and increased effort to perform tasks at the level we're used to.

The passage above is a good example of fatigue. Elijah, a mighty prophet of God, had just experienced a remarkable victory in 1 Kings 18, where God displayed His power by defeating the prophets of Baal. Yet, in 1 Kings 19, we find him fleeing for his life after Jezebel's threat. Exhausted and overwhelmed, Elijah prayed for death, unable to see beyond his fatigue and despair. Despite his feelings, God met him with compassion, sending an angel to provide food, water, and rest. Elijah's response shows that even after great victories, we can grow weary. Yet, God's care is constant.

For instance, Elijah encountered God in the wilderness in a gentle whisper, not in the dramatic wind, earthquake, or fire. God's soft approach reminds us that we might miss God's presence in moments of exhaustion because we're too overwhelmed to notice. Even when Elijah felt alone and defeated, God reassured him of His plan and the seven thousand faithful who had not bowed to Baal. This story teaches us to rest in God's provision, recognize

His guidance amidst the chaos, and remember that we are never alone, no matter how dire the circumstances!

This is serious, friends. Right now, suicide rates are at an all-time high. Regardless of how strong your faith may be, your mind, mental capacity, and overall well-being need attention. If you have been feeling depressed, it's crucial to seek therapy and medication and stay connected to your faith community. Ensure you're feeding your spirit by getting the Word in your daily study, learning from your church, and engaging in platforms like this Faith Fire community. A steady diet of the Word equips us when life gets tough. So, remember to feed your faith!

Especially if you're in a transitional season, communities like these are available to strengthen your faith, mind, and heart so the enemy doesn't wear you out with fatigue. Life can be overwhelming, and we've seen prominent figures like world-renowned chefs, fashion icons, comedians, and entertainers succumb to the weight of it by suicide (which, although tragic, is not the answer)! Your mind can deceive you into thinking it's over, your enemies have won, or your battle is lost before it has begun. However, God is faithful in restoring you if you bring Him your fatigue in exchange for His rest. We need you strong and well, so please lean on Him for encouragement!

For example, in Scripture, we see how Elijah rested after reaching the end of his strength. God sent angels to provide food and care, proving that sometimes we need to pause and reset. Rest, nourishment, and quiet times are essential, mainly when fatigue dulls your ability to hear from God. When the noise of life becomes too much, get still, play worship music, and let God minister to your spirit. The enemy of your soul seeks to wear you out, but you don't have to be a victim of fragmented or fatigued faith. Today, let your faith begin to heal. Stand firm on God's promises, whether this Word is for now or a future season. Be intentional about spending time with Him because life's battles are won when we draw near Him for strength. Not only do we need to pray and talk to God, but we also need to be attentive to His answers.

One final takeaway from this Scripture is that God is sending help. For some, He sends reinforcements; for others, He sends a successor. Someone needs to hear this: your ministry and legacy will not fail. The enemy may be wearing you down because you feel like everything rests on you–that you have to do it, stay in it, and carry it all alone. Some of you think you can't let anyone help you, but God is sending people to assist you. Delegation works when you entrust the right tasks to the right people. God is sending "destiny helpers" to help you fulfill your purpose on Earth. You must use discernment and wisdom but also accept that you can't do this alone. Without help, you risk burning out.

To those who feel overwhelmed, seeking help and allowing others to help you is okay. You need support, whether you're a single parent, a caregiver, or someone with a demanding role. I've been there, so I understand the struggle. I had to learn the importance of leaning on my parents and trusted friends to lighten my load. Doing so made all the difference.

If you've been burdened by attempting to do something hard alone, it's time to ask for and accept help. Spend time with God, pray, and He will bring the right people into your life. He may remind you of people from your past or place new ones in your path. *Some seasons require you to push through alone, but others demand support.* It's critical to know the difference. Don't let pride or ego rob you of the help God has already appointed for you.

You weren't designed to live or fulfill your calling in isolation. Trust that God has provided the resources you need, and don't let your purpose fail because you refuse to let go or accept assistance.

Fatigue can manifest in many ways that impact our performance in life and safety. When you notice specific signs such as doing tasks incorrectly, struggling to manage multiple tasks, frequently forgetting things, double booking meetings, etc, you have become a victim of fatigue. You may begin to work on autopilot without fully thinking, fall asleep briefly, or feel constantly tired or prone to yawning. Fatigue happens when we haven't appropriately rested yet keep pushing forward despite our slip-hanging. In these situations, we are fatigued, and it is time to take a mandatory rest.

When I become increasingly irritated without warning, I notice that my behaviors change, like frustration with tasks or difficulty concentrating. Again, these are all signs that I am not receiving adequate rest. Other warning signs include being uncommunicative, overlooking risks, taking unusual risks, or responding slowly. It's important to remember that we often underestimate our level of fatigue, thus making it crucial to stay vigilant and address these symptoms when they arise.

The enemy of our souls is banking on this to inflict pain when we are most vulnerable, depleted, and fatigued. Low energy levels can cause depression to creep in and take over subtly. It can happen to anyone, including seasoned believers, with a list of breakthroughs. There are some situations we face that are weightier, complex, and altogether below the belt that can cause us to succumb to a fatigued faith crisis or, worse, become suicidal, like Elijah. Let's be grateful that even then, God is sensitive enough to send help to strengthen us when we are fatigued in our faith.

Allow me to share a personal story to demonstrate. In the second year of the Earn Your Leisure conference, I was fortunate to attend it with a girlfriend. Over the weekend, we heard many incredible speakers, most of whom were speakers of color and celebrities or influencers. However, some of my most memorable moments came from an unexpected speaker: Dan Cathy, son of Truett Cathy and founder of Chick-fil-A. He gave one of the most honest, eye-opening perspectives I had ever heard regarding succession. I am unsure what I expected, but he started by dropping gems. I will give you a few:

- "Economic mobility is one of the toughest things to change; the stats bear this out because only four percent of poor people can rise above poverty." This research is why our business is so important, and we take it so seriously: our jobs are what we are "paid for," but our calling is what we were "made for."

- Though our family owns a franchise, not every member is involved in operations. While our ownership is not optional, neither is our stewardship.

- We take management very seriously and vet all prospects. We run it this way because in family businesses, only a third of family-owned businesses survive to the second generation. Chick-fil-A (at the time of this event) has 350 thousand employees.

- EVERYONE learns the same methods for their legendary sandwich prep: *"Pickles on a sandwich–date, but don't mate."* This example refers to how the epic chicken sandwich is made.

Dan Cathy went on to talk about creating an exceptional experience for their restaurant guests. The famous second-mile service is a cornerstone of the chain's popularity. He stated that service is a game changer. He gave the example of going to a 5-star hotel. He noted that the toilet paper edge is shaped like a triangle and demonstrated how easy it is to do it. The point was that something so simple could leave a significant impact. He expressed how every business should focus on the consumer experience and go above and beyond.

Another example of excellence Dan used was in comparison to music. An orchestra and conductor will play music and a score. They don't dummy down the music; they select the right musicians. Dan stressed the importance of determining the *right* people for a job. As business leaders and life leaders, having the most efficient people on board is essential.

Likewise, the best transitions occur when the next leader is **ready to lead**, not when the current leader is prepared to leave. This point stood out to me the most. Working in the religious non-profit space for twenty years, I cannot say how many people I have seen mess this transition up. As a result, some leaders have jumped out and started ministries without the benefit and guidance of wise counsel.

In the same way, some older leaders have slowly killed churches because they've refused to allow younger leaders to transition to the front end while they transition back. Dan Cathy realized the art of succession after his son exemplified leadership during COVID-19. The pandemic showed him that his son was ready to lead and was the perfect person to take them to the next level; even though he could stay on, wisdom dictated that he should not.

Cathy's words left a long-lasting impression on me regarding fatigue. We must be careful not to stay in certain seasons of our lives too long. There is an appointed time for everything. It will wear us out if we try to hold on to things we are supposed to release past the appointed time. At the end of 1 Kings 19, God says, "If one doesn't bring judgment, the next will, and if that one doesn't, the next one will. Whoever escapes the sword of Hazael, Jehu will be put to death, and whoever escapes Jehu, Elisha will be put to death."

Do you think *everybody's* going to bow to Baal? Perhaps not. You may think you're the last one standing with faith, but that is false. God is with you. *We* are with you. As the saying goes, "Stronger is He that is within me (and you) than he that's within the world." Together, we can conquer our most significant challenges. Through God, we can defeat *fatigued faith.*

If you are reading this, you may require significant rest, help, and a support system. Someone else may need God's divine presence. They may need to turn off their phone and get into a quiet place. Maybe they need to put on some worship music and praise God. They may need to be still and hear from God. Wherever you are in your fatigued faith journey, the time to take action is now. Confess it, share it, and be still because God didn't come in an earthquake, fire, or wind but in a still, small voice.

I pray this devotional has blessed you, and if it has, please share it with others. And whatever you do, get rest. Don't let fatigued faith make you want to go before your time. Rest in Jesus' name. Amen. Love you guys!

FATIGUED FAITH NOTES:

1. **Your enemy's talk game is strong, but your God is more powerful!** Don't allow misconception to trump all the victories you have already experienced. In 1 Kings 18, Elijah had just seen all the prophets killed. God had shown up and showed out in less than twenty-four hours. He was worn out in the camp because his enemy used threats to wear him down and fatigue his faith. Elijah had the wrong impression.

2. **You will want to die if you don't grasp fatigued faith**. Suicide right now is at an all-time high. In the last few years, we have seen a world-renowned chef, a fashion empress, an award-winning comedian, and one of this generation's best dancers and entertainers all take their lives. Life will drag you if you let it. Your mind can play tricks on you and convince you that IT IS OVER. Your brain can make you think that your enemies have already won and that the battle is over before it begins, but God will restore you if you give Him your fatigued faith. He will exchange it for rest. Then He will send help.

3. **God spoke to Elijah in the quiet and the calm.** God is saying something today, which may be in the softest, not the loudest way. We must intentionally spend time with Him, praying and being attentive to His answers.

4. **God has dispatched divine assistance; help is on the way!** For some of you, He sends reinforcement; for others, He sends a successor. I don't know who this is for, but your ministry and your legacy will not fall to the ground. God has appointed another to pick up where you have left off, so rest in Him. Sometimes, our egos choke our lives out because we believe we are the only ones who can do it all.

FATIGUED FAITH PRAYER

Dear Lord,

I pray that You will speak to Your children today, bringing peace that surpasses our understanding. Please remove any doubts or second thoughts we may have about our purpose. Remind us that Your will is perfect and transitions are necessary for growth. Amen.

DAY *FIVE*
Frayed Faith

Frayed | | frād | *adjective*
Unraveled, shredded, or worn at the edge; worried, upset, annoyed, coming apart, showing the effects of strain.

Frayed Faith
Scripture Lesson

Mark 9:14-29, NIV

"**14** *When they came to the other disciples, they saw a large crowd around them and the teachers of the law arguing with them.* **15** *As soon as all the people saw Jesus, they were overwhelmed with wonder and ran to greet Him.*

16 *"What are you arguing with them about?" He asked.*

17 *A man in the crowd answered, "Teacher, I brought You my son, who is possessed by a spirit that has robbed him of speech.* **18** *Whenever it seizes him, it throws him to the ground. He foams at the mouth, gnashes his teeth and becomes rigid. I asked Your disciples to drive out the spirit, but they could not."*

19 *"You unbelieving generation," Jesus replied, "how long shall I stay with you? How long shall I put up with you? Bring the boy to Me."*

20 *So they brought him. When the spirit saw Jesus, it immediately threw the boy into a convulsion. He fell to the ground and rolled around, foaming at the mouth.*

21 *Jesus asked the boy's father, "How long has he been like this?"*

"From childhood," he answered. **22** "It has often thrown him into fire or water to kill him. But if You can do anything, take pity on us and help us."

23 "If You can?" said Jesus. "Everything is possible for one who believes."

24 Immediately, the boy's father exclaimed, "I do believe; help me overcome my unbelief!"

25 When Jesus saw that a crowd was running to the scene, He rebuked the impure spirit. "You deaf and mute spirit," He said, "I command you, come out of him and never enter him again."

26 The spirit shrieked, convulsed him violently, and came out. The boy looked so much like a corpse that many said, "He's dead."

27 But Jesus took him by the hand and lifted him to his feet, and he stood up. **28** After Jesus had gone indoors, His disciples asked Him privately, "Why couldn't we drive it out?"

29 He replied, "This kind can come out only by prayer."

We are here together, attacking fragments and fixing fractured faith. On day five, we are rolling through this and addressing **frayed faith**. This type of faith is unraveled, shredded, or worn at the edges. Frayed faith reveals itself in worry, frustration, and strain. Frayed faith sometimes feels tattered and worn; it's still there but stretched to its limits.

For example, the father in the above passage was desperate. He was so desperate that he believed those who walked with Jesus carried the same power and authority as Jesus Himself, which can be dangerous. Yet, even in desperation, the father was honest about his doubt. He admitted, "I do believe; help me overcome my unbelief!" Jesus met him in that vulnerable moment, healing his son and restoring his faith.

This Scripture teaches that frayed faith doesn't disqualify us. Instead, it's an opportunity for God to step in and strengthen us where we are weak. The key is acknowledging where we need help–just like the father in the story did. We cannot erroneously assume that just because people walk with Jesus, say they know Jesus, or quote Scripture, they automatically carry the power of the Lord within them. We cannot assume that such people can bring healing, help us see the Lord in a transformative way, or guide us to a more profound spiritual breakthrough.

However, at the same time, Jesus Himself said the Disciples *should* have been able to heal the boy. So, while the father's assumption was technically incorrect, the Disciple's abilities *should* have been more efficient. Yet, they lacked the faith to act, so Jesus rebuked them.

Imagine the father's situation: his faith was already shredded. He brought his son to Jesus' last known place, desperate for a miracle. When he arrived, Jesus wasn't there. Instead, he encountered the Disciples, the "assistant pastors" or "team leads," so to speak. They told him they could help, but they failed. Now, there's arguing, commotion, and frustration. Then Jesus shows up, asking, "What's going on?"

The father steps forward, exhausted and heartbroken, and explains that this has been his son's condition for so long. He'd tried everything, and nothing had worked. His faith was frazzled, worn to a thread. But Jesus was now on the scene. When the father asked Jesus if there was anything He could do to help, Jesus challenged him with a response that shifted the focus: *everything is possible for the one who believes.*

The moment reminds us of **fully functional faith**, which operates in complete belief. It's like when God asked the prophet, "Can these bones live?" and the prophet humbly replied, "Lord, only You know." Similarly, this father, though desperate and broken, responds honestly to Jesus: "I believe; help me overcome my unbelief."

The father's prayer is one of the most transparent prayers in Scripture, and we can learn from it. Church leaders may fail us. Bosses may fail us. Politicians may fail us. Even those closest to us may let us down. But **God never fails!** Sometimes, we open our hands and hearts to believe, yet still feel the strain of frayed faith. We must cry out to the Father in those moments: ***"Lord, help my frayed, frazzled, fragile faith. I need it made whole. No more fragments–I need my faith restored."***

When we bring our honest prayers to God, no matter how tattered our faith feels, He hears us. Just as Jesus healed the man's son despite the father's imperfect faith, God can mend the broken threads of our faith. The father admitted how long the suffering had persisted–*"Since childhood,"* he said. Likewise, some challenges in our lives are so long-standing and painful that they feel like they could destroy us. The boy's condition had even thrown him into fire and water, threatening his life.

And isn't it just like the enemy to cause chaos when Jesus shows up? The enemy knows his time is limited. Like Jezebel's words to Elijah, he threatens: "By this time tomorrow, I will destroy you." But no matter how loudly the enemy roars, his defeat is inevitable when Jesus steps in. It doesn't matter how frayed your faith is, how exhausted you feel, or how long you've been battling. When Jesus shows up, healing and restoration follow. Your situation may seem hopeless, but God can take the things that traumatize you and turn them around for your good. No matter how worn your faith may be, it can be mended. Let the Master Physician make you whole again. **When Jesus shows up, healing isn't just possible–it's inevitable.**

The truth is that trusting God with life transitions can significantly feel risky when our faith is frayed. We often fear what might happen if we let go. *Will the next person be ready? Will the ministry, business, or family falter without us?* These questions come from a place of uncertainty. Still, God calls us to trust Him fully: *"Trust in the Lord with all your heart and lean not on your own understanding; in all your ways submit to Him, and He will make your paths straight" (Proverbs 3:5-6).*

Most importantly, the Word of God shows us a better way to submit to leadership. God, in His wisdom, demonstrates the art of succession. Though fully capable, Moses didn't take the Israelites into the Promised Land; instead, he prepared Joshua to lead. Eventually, Elijah passed the mantle to Elisha. In the same way, Jesus spent years mentoring His Disciples so they could continue His ministry after His ascension.

When we trust God to guide the process, He strengthens our frayed faith and teaches us the beauty of surrender. Leadership isn't about holding on tightly to authority. Instead, we should be faithful stewards of the time, gifts, and people God has placed in our care.

If your faith feels frayed today, ask yourself: *is God calling me to trust Him in a transition? Am I clinging to something He is asking me to release?* Or *is He asking me to step into a leadership role with boldness?* When we embrace God's timing, He weaves the frayed threads of our faith into a beautiful testimony of His faithfulness.

Remember, your calling is what you were *made for,* and God has already prepared the way. Surrender to Him and watch how He uses you to make an eternal impact. Call on Jesus, saying, "*Lord, do it.*" For anyone feeling weak in their faith today, I want to encourage you. I'm standing with you in faith if you're looking for a job. I believe the job you've been waiting for, the one you've been praying for–the link between where you are now and the destination God has for you–is on the way. And it is not just *any* job; *the* job you've been specifically waiting for is coming alive for you right now.

For those praying for healing, whatever is weighing you down, whatever sickness or struggle you face will be lifted off you. You're worn out, afraid, and tired, but the Lord is on the scene. The Master Physician has shown up, asking you, "Do you believe?" For those who believe but feel overwhelmed by doubt, I pray that God helps you overcome your unbelief. He's doing it right now.

Starting today, we're letting go of frayed faith–no more being tattered or torn apart. In Jesus' name, we are made whole. The Master Physician is in the room, healing, restoring, and helping us overcome our unbelief. Believe it is so. Count it as done. Go in peace, be blessed, and walk in the fullness of God's promises. I'll see you on Day 6. Love you!

FRAYED FAITH NOTES

1. **Sometimes, your faith can get so frayed that it shows up tattered**. It's there but worn at the ends. The father was desperate. He was so desperate that he assumed the people who walked with Jesus had His power and authority, which was dangerous.

2. **There is someone depending on your faith.** The Father expected the Disciples to help Him and His Son. Jesus confirmed that the Disciples SHOULD have been able to drive the spirit out, but their faith was not strong enough. Their lack of faith caused Jesus to rebuke them.

3. **It is crucial that your faith adds and does not subtract from the faith of others.** The frayed faith of the disciples caused the father's faith to unravel. So, the father's faith is shredded by the time Jesus arrives on the scene. The Master Physician shows up, and the weary father asks Jesus "*if*" He can do anything for them. But Jesus puts it back on the father: "*I can do anything for him who believes.*"

4. **When our faith gets low, we can be honest with Jesus.** The father responded honestly to confessing frayed faith: "I believe but help my unbelief." We must be truthful with our Creator. Occasionally, the church fails us. A leader fails us. A spouse fails us. A child or parent may fail us. Heck, we even

fail ourselves! But God will never fail, and He is standing there with open arms, ready to help the unbelief of our fried, frayed, and frazzled faith.

5. **Some demons, strongholds, or issues only break with prayer and fasting**. One way to repair your frayed faith is by turning down your plate. There is a resource guide at the end of this book that outlines consecration and fasting for you.

FRAYED FAITH PRAYER

Heavenly Father,

I lift up everyone reading this devotional. For those whose faith is frayed and fragile, I pray You show up in a mighty way. I know You've already gone before us, Lord. You know the cries of our hearts and the needs of every person here.

God, we believe in You! We come to You, diligently seeking You wherever You may be found, and we trust that You will respond. We believe it's already done. Just as You cast out the demon from the boy and declared it would never return, we know You're delivering us from sickness, joblessness, financial struggles, and all other battles we face. We declare that when Your blessings come, they will never leave us. We will never be the same. God, we trust that You are already at work. It is done, and when You move, we will give You all the glory, all the honor, and all the praise!

Thank You for being the ultimate guide in all areas of our lives. When our faith feels frayed, and we're tempted to hold on to control, remind us to trust in Your timing. Help us to steward the roles You've given us and to raise others to lead with wisdom. Teach us to listen for Your voice and to step aside when it's time, knowing You have a more excellent plan. Strengthen our faith and use our lives to bring glory to You. In Jesus' mighty name, Amen.

<u>Special Bonus</u>: **Want to strengthen your frayed faith more? Check out the resource guide at the end of the book entitled, Consecration and Fasting!**

DAY SIX
Forced Faith

forced | fôrst | *adjective*
Compelled or involuntary; done out of necessity.

Forced Faith
Scripture Lesson

Jonah 2:1-10, NIV

"*1 From inside the fish Jonah prayed to the Lord his God. 2 He said: "In my distress I called to the Lord, and He answered me. From deep in the realm of the dead, I called for help, and You listened to my cry. 3 You hurled me into the depths, into the very heart of the seas, and the currents swirled about me; all Your waves and breakers swept over me. 4 I said, 'I have been banished from Your sight; yet I will look again toward Your holy temple.' 5 The engulfing waters threatened me, the deep surrounded me; seaweed was wrapped around my head. 6 To the roots of the mountains I sank down, the earth beneath barred me in forever. But You, Lord my God, brought my life up from the pit. 7 "When my life was ebbing away, I remembered You, Lord, and my prayer rose to You, to Your holy temple. 8 'Those who cling to worthless idols turn away from God's love for them. 9 But I, with shouts of grateful praise, will sacrifice to You. What I have vowed I will make good. I will say, 'Salvation comes from the Lord.'" 10 And the Lord commanded the fish, and it vomited Jonah onto dry land.*

ey guys! Day Six is here, and we are almost at the end of another challenge. I'm so excited you've been rocking with me this long! I pray this has been a blessing to you. So, let's dive into today's topic: forced faith. The word *forced* means to be compelled, involuntarily moved, or to do something out of necessity.

Before Jonah 2, we see a clear example of forced faith in Jonah 1. I did not include that Scripture above, but here is a summary. In chapter one, God gave Jonah clear instructions: go to Nineveh and deliver a message of repentance. But Jonah didn't want to obey. He believed the people of Nineveh didn't deserve God's mercy, and he knew that if they repented, God would forgive them. Instead of following God's command, Jonah decided to go in the opposite direction. He ignored his divine assignment.

It was pretty bold of Jonah to tell God "No." In comparison, it would be like receiving military orders and going AWOL instead. Yet, God created circumstances to force Jonah's faith in the right direction because of God's love for Jonah and the people. Jonah lacked the faith to obey. He didn't trust God or have the level of faith we discussed in this series. Jonah decided to do his own thing.

A lesson can be learned from Jonah's disobedience. When God has a call on your life, He will force your faith back in the right direction to save you. One thing I've learned in my 45, almost 46 years of life is this: God will do what it takes to get your attention. If you're His child and He's protecting you, your rebellion can only go so far. It's a sign of His love when He decides to intervene rather than let us go our own way.

However, God's grace doesn't mean you have until eternity to repent. If His hand is on you, God will grab your attention in a way that leaves you no choice but to face your assignment. Many of you know you're being called, whether it be ministry, a career change, or something specific. Yet, you're running from it. Therefore, prepare yourself. Jesus will force your faith back in the right direction.

Think about what happened next to Jonah. He boarded a ship, planning a getaway. But soon, a storm arose. The sailors panicked, realizing their boat was about to sink. Then Jonah admitted he was the problem. When the sailors asked what to do next, Jonah told them to throw him overboard. At that moment, God could have let him die for his disobedience. But instead, He showed grace and created a situation to push Jonah toward obedience—*that's* the love of our Father.

Sometimes, discipline means writing sentences on a chalkboard, getting spanked by your parents, or losing privileges. Whatever the consequence, the objective is intended to teach obedience. Similarly, God sometimes forces circumstances to get us back on track. It's not voluntary. Before Jonah boarded that ship, before the storm raged, and even inside the whale, God gave him time to repent. Forced faith redirected Jonah to his assignment.

Likewise, if you're called by God and go astray, He provides grace and a window of opportunity to get back on track. He is drawing you back, preventing your current fracture from becoming a complete break. He wants you to fulfill your purpose. Sometimes, that means using you to bless people you don't even like. Can I get an *amen*?

And if you don't believe me, remember how God sent ravens to feed Elijah. Ravens don't like people, yet God used them to sustain His prophet. Have you been blessed by someone who didn't mean to help you? Jonah had an attitude because God wanted to save Nineveh. But God reminded him: *you don't get to decide that.* Let Jonah's rebellion be a reminder not to judge, move in arrogance, or reject God's assignments.

We're almost at the end of this challenge, and it has been a blessing to walk through it with you! If this has encouraged you, again, please tell someone about this devotional. Additionally, I would love to hear your testimony, so please send it to me! Your journey encourages and strengthens me, and I'm standing in faith with you that we will see the goodness of the Lord in the land of the living. Be blessed!

FORCED FAITH NOTES:

1. **God will get your attention.** Jonah thought he could outrun God's call, but he was mistaken. When you are chosen for a purpose, you can't outrun God.

2. **God will create situations to compel you to obey.** Sometimes, discipline comes in the form of *forced obedience*. For instance, when you were a kid and got punished, wrote sentences, or lost privileges, someone loved you enough to correct your behavior. God does the same for His children.

3. **God allows time and space for repentance.** When God calls you to an assignment, He wants you to fulfill it. Even if you're resistant, He gives you a window of opportunity to get back on track before it's too late. Don't wait until you're forced–choose to obey now! If you know God is calling you

to something, whether ministry, a career change, or a specific task–don't run. Trust Him. Say *"yes"* before you end up in a situation where your faith has to be forced back into place.

FORCED FAITH PRAYER:

Dear Lord,

We don't want God to force our faith back in the right direction. Please help us walk in obedience now. We receive the assignment You have given us and will obey without forced faith. Amen.

DAY SEVEN
Failed Faith

Failed | fāld | *adjective*
To fail to meet standards by neglect, to break down,
or to cease working well.

Failed Faith
Scripture Lesson

Genesis 19:15-26, NIV

"15 With the coming of dawn, the angels urged Lot, saying, "Hurry! Take your wife and your two daughters who are here, or you will be swept away when the city is punished."

16 When he hesitated, the men grasped his hand and the hands of his wife and of his two daughters and led them safely out of the city, for the Lord was merciful to them. 17 As soon as they had brought them out, one of them said, "Flee for your lives! Don't look back, and don't stop anywhere in the plain! Flee to the mountains or you will be swept away!"

18 But Lot said to them, "No, my lords, please! 19 Your servant has found favor in your eyes, and you have shown great kindness to me in sparing my life. But I can't flee to the mountains; this disaster will overtake me, and I'll die. 20 Look, here is a town near enough to run to, and it is small. Let me flee to it–it is very small, isn't it? Then my life will be spared."

21 He said to him, "Very well, I will grant this request too; I will not overthrow the town you speak of. 22 But flee there quickly, because I cannot do anything until you reach it." (That is why the town was called Zoar.) 23 By the time Lot reached Zoar, the sun had risen over the land. 24

*Then the Lord rained down burning sulfur on Sodom and Gomorrah–from the Lord out of the heavens. **25** Thus He overthrew those cities and the entire plain, destroying all those living in the cities–and also the vegetation in the land. **26** But Lot's wife looked back, and she became a pillar of salt."*

D ay Seven is here! Thank you for joining me on this faith journey. We've reached the final day of our devotional, and today's topic is centered around faith that has failed. Let's dive in!

As mentioned earlier, failing faith means being unable to meet the standard set, neglecting to do something, breaking down, or ceasing to function properly or work. When we examine Genesis 19:15-26 more closely, we see that Lot hesitated, but God, in His mercy, intervened on behalf of the righteous. Then, angels took Lot and his family by the hand to lead them out of danger. Can we pause for a moment to see the love, intentionality, care, and concern that God demonstrated to Lot and his family? He didn't just send *any* angel–this angel had authority. He took Lot's hand to ensure he arrived safely and swiftly at the designated place.

You might be wondering: Does the evidence of forced faith from the previous chapter play a role here? If you are thinking along those lines, you are on the right track. The faith-filled days you've experienced so far serve as building blocks in your spiritual journey. We'll explore that idea further later; for now, let's continue by returning to the account.

Lot's family received clear instructions: *flee, don't look back, don't stop.* Yet Lot's wife looked back. She disobeyed and was turned to a pillar of salt–on the verge of deliverance but losing it all. The key is that hesitation or looking back can cost us blessings and safety.

It's easy to look back when facing something new. Resist nostalgia or fear–forward movement with God leads to better things. Remember, losing faith can cost everything, and you've come too far to lose it now.

ANOTHER FAILED FAITH HOUSEWIFE OF THE NEW TESTAMENT

Lot's wife was not alone in failed faith. In Job 2:9-10, Job's wife said, "Are you still maintaining your integrity? Curse God and die!" Job replied, "You are talking like a foolish woman. Shall we accept good from God and not trouble?" Despite his suffering, Job did not sin. Afterward, we hear nothing more about her; commentators differ on her fate, but she isn't mentioned when Job's fortunes change. Though Lot's story was different from Job's wife, there are similarities to note. Let's briefly rewind to see how we got here. Lot was Abraham's nephew. He separated from Abraham and picked a land that became filled with evil. Angels later came to Lot, warning him that the city was wicked and God was set to destroy it. Yet, because God is merciful, He made a way for Lot and his family to escape.

The angels gave clear instructions: *don't do this, don't do that, and don't look back.* Unfortunately, Lot's wife couldn't hold onto her faith. She needed a future-focused faith in God's promises and a new direction, but she froze, looked back, and became a pillar of salt. Job's wife had lost her children, her home, and her livelihood–*everything*. Her losses felt like a storm that destroyed all in its path. In the aftermath, only Job, his wife, and a few servants were left to mourn. In this painful place, Job's wife was at her lowest. Her faith failed. She looked at her husband, a man of God, and saw him keeping his integrity despite all they had lost. So she said, "Curse God and die." It was horrible advice, spoken out of pain and exhaustion.

Job ignored her advice. Despite his suffering, Job was steadfast: *"You are talking like a foolish woman. Shall we accept good from God and not trouble?"* Job knew life brings blessings and hardship and never spoke sinfully. The lesson: when loved ones advise out of hurt or failed faith, stay rooted in what's true about God. Job's refusal to curse God during loss demonstrates unshakeable faith–the main point of this devotional. When faith is weak, resources are available to help restore it.

Scripture shows both faithfulness and failure, offering lessons to follow or avoid. Choices bring blessings or consequences. Failed faith resembles Lot's wife looking back or Job's wife's hopeless advice. Our challenge: hold to God's promises, keep moving forward despite pain or uncertainty, and trust Him with the future.

To reinforce this point, consider another example: in the Garden of Eden, Eve's faith faltered as she held onto the forbidden fruit and shared it with Adam. Instead of taking responsibility, Adam also partook, and their failure to stand firm in faith allowed sin to enter the world.

Proverbs 31 describes the ideal wife and mother, outlining qualities all believers can develop as they build legacies. While the Bible honors women like Esther and Ruth, others fell short of their standards. The failed faith of Lot's wife and Job's wife illustrates how not to react in adversity and highlights the importance of communicating faith and hope, rather than negativity, during trials. To stand in times of trouble, we need defensive tactics ready.

Scripture warns we cannot avoid pain or challenges, but we can activate our faith to stand firm and resist the enemy. I have three for you to use in your battles with your faith is failing.

FAILED FAITH TACTICS

Let's break down some of the tactics we must be ready to deploy:

Tactic #1 - Accept responsibility for the generations following our example. As parents, guardians, or mentors, our presence and faithfulness play a critical role in protecting and guiding future generations. We cannot let our faith falter. We must remain steadfast in fulfilling the roles God has called us to and ensure that we leave a legacy of faith for those who come after us.

Tactic #2-Learn from the faith warriors that came before us. Studying the failed faith of those who came before us helps us learn from their mistakes and make wiser choices. I tell my children, "Make new mistakes." Mistakes like choosing a poor romantic partner, overspending in college, or mistaking frenemies for friends–these are lessons your family learned, so you don't have to. We already carried that burden; you can just take the lesson. Similarly, let's examine the giants of faith in Scripture and in Kingdom Culture. We can observe their lives, learn from them, and apply those lessons to ourselves and those we lead.

Tactic #3- Our bodies must be battle-ready. You can't win if you can't war! In life, you will encounter various battles: spiritual, mental, emotional, and financial, but one of the toughest as we age is the physical battle. It is mission-critical that we take care of our bodies. If you follow me on social media, you know I've been going to the gym. Let me be clear: I am not a "gym rat." Even though my husband, who is now working in real estate, is also a certified trainer, the gym is not my favorite place. However, I go because it's essential for my mental health, helps keep my mind sharp, and gives me time with the Lord. Additionally, staying physically strong is essential for accomplishing everything I want to achieve. I want to be here as long as possible for my kids, my husband, and my parents.

I understand that to be present for my family, I must take care of the temple God has given me. If I neglect my health, my well-being will suffer and potentially lead to death. I would miss opportunities to impart wisdom to my children, be present for my parents, and show love to my spouse. Taking care of myself enables me to make meaningful contributions to my family's well-being.

In general, women often take care of everyone except themselves. Still, they must learn to prioritize their health and wellness (me included). Just as the advice given before a plane takes off is to put on your own oxygen mask first, so that you can effectively care for others, we must do the same.

Though this book was written for men and women, I encourage all readers to remember the critical roles of matriarchs. These roles are often singularly tied to the household's heritage, legacy, wisdom, and stability. When women take care of themselves and embrace these roles with strength and intention, they position themselves to make a lasting impact on their families and future generations. And the same is true for men, our patriarchs. If men allow society to convince them that their only contribution is financial, they work themselves to the bone and miss out on instilling critical values in the generations following them.

FAILED FAITH RECAP

Over the past seven days, we have been on a journey to understand fractured faith, its challenges, and its restoration. We have explored stories from the Bible that remind us of the faithfulness and failures of God's people. From Lot's wife's disobedience to Job's wife's faulty advice, we have seen how critical it is to guard our faith during life's trials. Faith affects not only us but our households, relationships, and the legacies we leave behind.

Through this devotional, we've learned that God always provides a way of escape, walks with us through seasons of destruction, and mercifully offers us opportunities to realign our hearts. Even when life is uncertain, we are reminded that God remains God, unchanging, ever-present, and faithful in every season. It is essential to uphold our faith, resist discouragement, and trust His promises. Why? Because He has equipped us for every assignment.

Additionally, these stories remind us of the consequences of hesitation, disobedience, and failing to trust in God's instructions. They challenge us to fully commit to what God calls us to do, while letting go of anything He tells us to release. This devotional has challenged us to assess our faith, strengthen our resolve, and step into the future with unwavering trust in God. As we conclude this challenge, let us commit to being intentional in our prayers, wise in our actions, and steadfast in our belief that God will never forsake us. Whether in our homes, workplaces, or communities, we are called to be examples of faith in action.

FAILED FAITH NOTES

1. **God will provide a way of escape.** Trust God's timing, even when you can't understand it. It is very easy to fall into the trap of looking back when God is doing a new thing in our lives. You must resist this urge to go back to the familiar when God is bringing you out! It can cost you everything, and you cannot afford to lose it all.

2. **God will walk you through destruction to save you.** The challenge for us is to hold on tightly to God's promises through moments of pain, fatigue, or uncertainty and move forward in faith, trusting Him. In Job's case, this took years, and he experienced excruciating pain in his body, mind, and soul. In the end, he received double provision and family by the mercy of God, and so did his wife!

3. **The consequences of your sin can affect generations after you.** We must remain steadfast in fulfilling the roles God has called us to and ensure that we leave a legacy of faith for those who come after us. Half of the battles emerge from nowhere and are rooted in the sins of past generations. But I declare over you today: you will overcome by the blood of the Lamb and the Word of your testimony!

FAILED FAITH PRAYER

Dear Heavenly Father,

Your Word does not return unto us void. Thank you for providing us with examples of failed faith in Scripture, so that we can avoid similar pitfalls. Forgive us for the times we have fallen into temptation and short of Your blessing. Please lead us to the path to righteousness and keep us focused on Your will. In Jesus' name, we pray. Amen

CONCLUSION

YOUR FRAGMENTS ARE NOW YOUR FOUNDATION—LET'S BUILD

L isten, family—we didn't spend these seven days picking up pieces just to put them in a pretty box on a shelf. No, ma'am. You've done the hard work. You've named your fractures, faced your fears, and let God speak truth into those tender places. You've stopped pretending everything was fine when it wasn't. That's not just growth—that's courage with a capital C.

But here's what I know about you, and here's what God knows about you: You weren't created to stay in recovery mode. Those fragments you've been gathering? They're not souvenirs from your survival story—they're the raw materials for your next kingdom assignment.

Future Forward Faith: Believing God Right Now for What's Next is where we shift from mending to momentum. This isn't about adding another devotional to your collection. This is about taking everything God just restored in you and aiming it at the future He's already preparing.

We're going from *"Lord, help me make it through"* to *"Lord, show me how to make it count."* From *"God, fix my faith"* to *"God, use my faith to fix what's broken around me."*

It's time to go from managing your fragments to maximizing your future. In that next journey together, we're getting strategic. We're picking one area where God is calling you to activate—maybe it's that business idea you've been sitting on, that ministry you keep dreaming about, or that generational cycle you're ready to break. We're going to create kingdom strategies that turn those 3 AM prayers into 9 AM action plans. We're building the kind of faith that doesn't just believe God can—it partners with Him while He does.

Because here's the truth: Your fractures taught you dependence, but your future needs your participation. God didn't heal those broken places just so you could feel better. He healed them so you could BE better—for your family, for your community, for the kingdom assignment that's been waiting on your wholeness. The systems are shaking. The world is shifting. And God needs activated believers who've done their healing work and are ready to do His kingdom work. That's you. Yes, YOU—the one who just spent seven days letting God put you back together.

Now it's time to let Him put you to work.

So, here's my invitation—no, here's my challenge:

If you're tired of faith that just helps you cope and ready for faith that helps you conquer...

If you're done asking, "Why me?" and ready to declare "Use me!"...

If you know there's something with your name on it in this next season...

Then ***Future Forward Faith*** is your next step. Not someday. Not when you feel more ready. Not after you've got it all together (because honey, that day isn't coming).

Your fragments are healed. Your foundation is solid. Your future is calling. I'll see you on the next page—because your best is yet to come, and we're going to activate every bit of faith it takes to get there.

Remember: You didn't survive your fractures to play it safe with your future. Let's go build something beautiful with these restored pieces.

Ready to move forward? Your future is waiting, and so am I.

Activated and expecting, Rainah

RESOURCE GUIDE:
Consecration and Fasting

YOUR SPIRITUAL POWER-UP FOR STRENGTHENING FRAYED FAITH

This resource guide serves as your companion to Day 5: Frayed Faith. Why? Because sometimes you need more than a daily reading to break through. You need a battle plan. Remember the desperate father who cried out, "I do believe; help me overcome my unbelief!" Remember when Jesus told His disciples, "This kind can come out only by prayer and fasting?" Well, He wasn't just making conversation. He was handing us a spiritual power tool. That's why we've created this comprehensive guide as a supplement to your devotional journey–as a spiritual power-up to help you navigate frayed faith.

Your faith may feel tattered, worn down by life's challenges. It could stem from disappointment or waiting for promises to be fulfilled. That's why we're highlighting consecration and fasting. They're not rituals to check off, but tools for restoring fractured faith.

Now that you know why we're here, let's clarify what consecration truly means. Consecration is formally dedicating yourself to God. It's like drawing a holy circle around your life and saying, "God, this is Yours." We're fasting and praying to clear the clutter and hear God more clearly. Consecration isn't about perfection. It's about being available to receive what God wants to pour into your life.

THE REAL DEAL ABOUT FASTING

Fasting is denying yourself something important for a spiritual purpose. It's not because God needs you to be hungry, but because you need clarity through intentional sacrifice. Jesus fasted. His Disciples fasted. And Jesus straight-up said we should fast too (Matthew 9:15). This isn't a suggestion from heaven–it's a strategy for breakthrough. When you fast, you quiet your flesh and amplify God's voice through the Holy Spirit, allowing for a deeper connection and understanding. You receive instructions, answers, and yes, even miracles with stunning clarity as your distractions fade. You prove to your flesh that your spirit is boss (take that, temptation!), building spiritual discipline and inner strength.

You literally detox your body while detoxing your soul. The main goal? Drawing nearer to God by removing obstacles and sharpening your spiritual focus. Every benefit–greater clarity, stronger discipline, physical renewal–supports that purpose.

YOUR FASTING GAME PLAN

Start Where You Are
(Not Where You Think You Should Be)

We're all at different places with God. Your fast should challenge you but not break you. Pray and follow the Holy Spirit, not what others are doing. Here's where the rubber meets the road. Before you fast:

1. Pray about the type of fast God wants you to undertake.

2. Decide how much time each day you'll devote to prayer and reading God's Word.

3. Write it down (yes, actually write it–commitments in your head don't count).

4. Tell someone who will hold you accountable (and pray for you, not judge you).

DO IT SAFELY
(BECAUSE GOD CARES ABOUT YOUR HEALTH)

Listen, your concerned loved ones aren't wrong when they worry about your health during a fast. If done properly, fasting can bless you both spiritually and physically. But let's be smart about this:

Red Flags: If you have tumors, cancer, blood diseases, diabetes, or heart disease, include your doctor in your fasting decisions. If you're on medication, talk to your doctor before changing anything. This isn't a lack of faith–it's a matter of wisdom.

Nursing or pregnant: You're already sacrificing for life. Here are some alternatives (with doctor approval): a modified Daniel fast, avoiding sweets and desserts, no red meat, or fasting from non-food activities (social media, Netflix, etc.).

Medical Disclaimer: If you are pregnant or a nursing mother, have a current or pre-existing medical or mental condition, or work a strenuous, physically demanding job, you should NOT do a strict fast or perform strenuous exercise. Everyone, especially those listed above, should fast under the recommendation or supervision of a doctor. If you experience any physical or mental complications, you should immediately seek medical attention.

TYPES OF FASTS
(CHOOSE YOUR ADVENTURE)

1. **Total Fast ("Complete/Absolute")**

   a. **What it is:** Drinking only liquids–typically water with light juices as an option.

   b. **Best for:** Short durations, experienced fasters, specific breakthrough needs.

   c. **Reality check:** This is intense. Start small if you're new to this.

2. **Partial Fast**

   a. **What it is:** Abstaining from food during specific times (like 6:00 am to 3:00 pm or sunup to sundown).

   b. **Options include:**

      i.   Sunup to sundown

      ii. One meal a day

      iii. Skipping specific meals

      iv. Eating only certain foods while drinking only water

   c. **Best for:** Working professionals, those new to fasting, and longer fasting periods.

3. **Selective Fast (The Daniel Fast)**

   a. **What it is:** Removing certain elements from your diet.

   b. **Cut out:** Meat, sweets, bread, caffeine, juice, refined sugars, and fried foods.

   c. **Keep:** Water, fruits, vegetables, whole grains.

   d. **Best for:** First-time fasters, health-conscious individuals, 21-day commitments.

4. **Media Fast**

   a. **What it is:** Abstaining from social media, TV, certain music, texting, and gaming.

   b. **Best for:** Those with health issues preventing food fasts, people addicted to their phones, and anyone needing to refocus.

   c. **Pro tip:** Replace scrolling with Scripture, Netflix with prayer, and Instagram with actual conversations.

5. **The Unconventional Fast**

   a. **What it is:** Fasting from negative forces in your life.

   b. **Examples:** Toxic relationships (limiting contact), sinful habits, bad attitudes, gossip, complaining.

   c. **Critical:** Replace what you remove with positive, Godly alternatives–church participation, healthy relationships, prayer, Bible reading.

PRACTICAL TIPS FOR FASTING SUCCESS

Water Is Your Best Friend

- Normal day: Drink half your body weight in ounces (160 lbs = 80 oz).

- Fasting day: Aim for 100 ounces minimum.

- Why: Helps detoxification, reduces hunger, maintains energy.

Navigate the Challenges

- First few days: Avoid food smells–they'll intensify hunger.

- Hunger pains: Turn them into prayer prompts.

- Usual TV time: Open your Bible instead.

- Social media urges: Text a friend encouragement or call someone to pray.

Exercise Wisely

- If eating during fast: Exercise normally (with doctor's approval).

- If total fasting: Skip the gym–this isn't the time to be a hero.

- Best option: Light walking while praying or listening to worship music.

WHEN HUNGER STRIKES (YOUR BATTLE PLAN)

When those hunger pains hit (and they will), here's your response strategy:

1. Acknowledge it: "Yes, I'm hungry. This is part of the process."
2. Redirect it: "This hunger reminds me of my hunger for God."
3. Use it: Pray specifically for the burdens that weigh on your heart.
4. Celebrate it: You're proving your spirit is stronger than your flesh!

THE FAMILY FACTOR

Don't fast alone if you don't have to! Include your family:

- Replace video game time with family devotions.
- Turn off devices and play board games together.
- Cook simple meals together (even if you're not eating them).
- Pray as a family for specific breakthroughs.

YOUR BREAKTHROUGH MINDSET

Remember this: Fasting isn't about impressing God with your sacrifice. It's about:

- Disconnecting from regular patterns to connect more closely with God.
- Creating space for God to work.
- Hitting the reset button on your soul.
- Celebrating God's goodness and mercy.
- Preparing your heart for all God desires to bring into your life.

THE BOTTOM LINE

Your frayed faith needs this. That worn-out, stretched-thin, hanging-by-a-thread faith needs the supernatural reinforcement that comes through consecration and fasting. Jesus said certain breakthroughs only come through prayer and fasting. Maybe your breakthrough has been waiting for you to take this step.

Don't let fear stop you. Don't let past failures discourage you. Don't let inexperience hold you back. Start where you are, choose a plan that works for you, and watch God meet you in that consecrated space. Your faith might be frayed, but it's not finished. Through consecration and fasting, those worn edges can become strong again. Those unraveled parts can be rewoven. That stretched-thin faith can become unshakeable.

It's time to stop talking about your frayed faith and start taking action. Pick your fast. Make your commitment. Set yourself apart. Your breakthrough is waiting on the other side of your obedience. Remember: God isn't looking for perfect fasters. He's looking for willing hearts. Yours qualifies. Now, let's attack those fragments and fix that fractured faith—one consecrated day at a time.

MAKE A COMMITMENT
(AND STICK TO IT)

Making commitments ahead of time is like setting your GPS; it helps you stay on track. When temptations come, you'll already know your destination. Write yours down below, and designate who you will share it with.

_____

_____

_____

_____

_____

_____

_____

_____

_____

_____

_____

_____

_____

_____

_____

_____

FINAL ENCOURAGEMENT

You've got this. More importantly, God's got you. Your willingness to consecrate yourself through fasting is already a victory. Every hunger pang is a prayer. Every sacrifice is seen. Every moment of consecration is moving you closer to a breakthrough. Welcome to the adventure of fasting. Your frayed faith is about to become fortified faith.